SOUND AND VISION

ROBIN KERROD

GRAFTON BOOKS

A Division of the Collins Publishing Group

LONDON GLASGOW
TORONTO SYDNEY AUCKLAND

Grafton Books
A Division of the Collins Publishing Group
8 Grafton Street, London W1X 3LA

Published by Grafton Books 1986

Copyright © Lionheart Books 1986

British Library Cataloguing in Publication Data
Kerrod, Robin
    Sound and vision.— (Dataworld; V.4)
    1. Home video systems — Juvenile literature
    2. Sound — Recording and reproducing —
    Equipment and supplies — Juvenile literature
    I. Title   II. Series
    621.388'332   TK6655.V5

    ISBN 0-246-12713-9

This book was conceived, edited and produced by
Lionheart Books
10 Chelmsford Square
London NW10 3AR

Editor Lionel Bender
Designer Malcolm Smythe
Picture Researcher Dee Robinson
Editorial Assistant Madeleine Bender
Illustrator Hayward Art Group
Typeset by Dorchester Typesetting Group Ltd.

Printed and bound in Italy by
New Interlitho, Milan

Contents

The Audiovisual Revolution

Nine hundred years ago, in 1086, William the Conqueror ordered a detailed survey of England. The results of the survey were written down in two volumes of what came to be called the Domesday Book. The Book gives details of land ownership and use, number of workers and so on in most English counties.

Domesday provides a unique record of English life in the AD 1080s. Today, another unique record of England and English life – but in the 1980s – is being prepared, this time by the BBC and the electronics firm Philips. It includes vast amounts of information in many different forms – maps, statistics, words and photos, enough to fill many volumes of a large encyclopedia.

But the information is not printed in books. It is recorded in code by the latest technology on just *two* video discs! The recording is made on the discs and played back by means of a laser beam. The discs display their words and pictures on a TV set or monitor. Their surface is protected by a perspex layer and will never wear out.

Dawn of the information age
Video discs are just one of the products that have ushered in an audiovisual (sound-vision) revolution.

Sound can now be reproduced on discs and tapes, and especially on laser-produced compact discs, so well that you might think it was the real thing.

Television enables us to watch live, in our homes, events happening practically anywhere in the world. It provides us with up-to-the-minute news and many hours of entertainment every day.

Linked into computer networks such as the viewdata system, the television can also be used as an electronic magazine containing anything from weather reports, tourist tips and cinema guides to recipes, games and quizzes – and even personal messages.

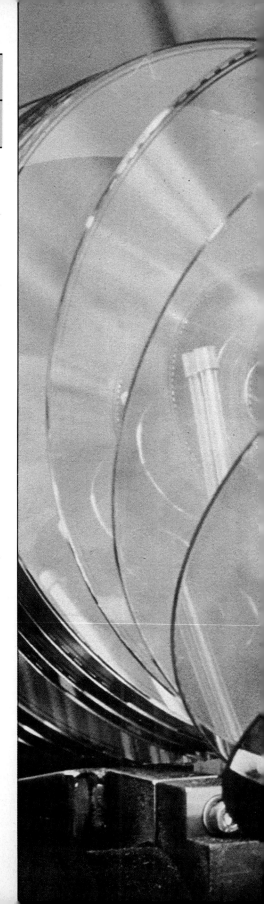

Compact discs are one of the latest ways of recording sound. They are virtually indestructible and are played back by being scanned by a laser beam.

Hi-fi

In 1877 the American Thomas Edison recited the nursery rhyme *Mary had a little lamb* into the horn of his latest invention, a contraption that he called the phonograph. The horn rested on, and moved along, a revolving cylinder covered in tin-foil. After his recitation he placed the horn at the beginning of the cylinder and rotated it again. Out from the horn came a distorted, but recognizable 'Mary had a little lamb'.

This was the beginning of the sound-recording, or audio industry, which can now bring the music of the greatest singers, groups and orchestras of the age right into our own living room. From that day to this, people have been striving constantly to improve the faithfulness, or fidelity, of sound reproduction.

Today, audio manufacturers record sounds in two ways, on disc and on magnetic tape. They use the latest technologies to ensure that these products are of the highest quality. When played back on the right equipment, they will produce sounds of high fidelity (hi-fi) nearly identical to the original.

Playback systems

There is a wealth of audio equipment available for playing back discs and tapes. There are portable tape recorders and disc record players for casual use, professional equipment for very high quality reproduction, and all-in-one music centres for the home. These music centres combine record

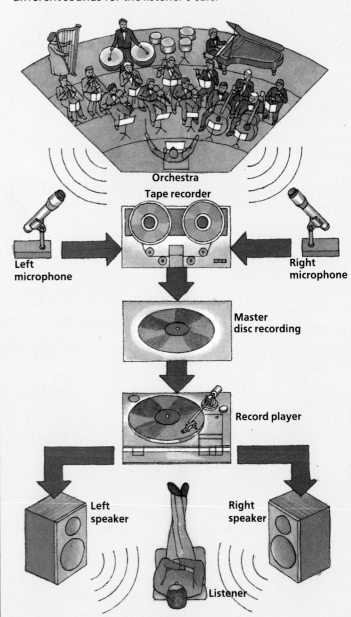

Listening in depth
Stereo recordings give music 'depth' by producing slightly different sounds for the listener's ears.

Orchestra

Tape recorder

Left microphone

Right microphone

Master disc recording

Record player

Left speaker

Right speaker

Listener

The signals from the two microphones are recorded as separate tracks on tape. From the tape a record disc is made. The two tracks are recorded separately on opposite sides of the groove in the disc. The needle of the record player picks up the 'left' and 'right' signals and feeds them to loudspeakers to the left and right of the listener.

player, tape recorder and usually a radio in a single unit; the three devices share the same electronic circuits and feed the same loudspeakers.

For the best hi-fi, however, record player, tape recorder and radio are kept separate. They each feed their signals into an electronic unit called an amplifier. This amplifies, or strengthens, the signals, which are then fed to the loudspeakers.

There are usually two loudspeakers, which should be placed to the right and left of the listener. The discs and tapes play back slightly different 'right' and 'left' sounds to the two speakers. These sounds have been recorded from positions to the right and left of the people making the recording.

The effect of listening to the different sounds from the right and left loudspeakers is to give the sound 'depth'. We call this effect stereophonic, or stereo. In stereo, we can hear the sounds of different instruments in an orchestra coming from different directions, just as we would if we were listening to the orchestra live.

For even more realistic listening, some hi-fi systems offer quadrophonic sound. This comes from four loudspeakers arranged two to the front and two to the rear of the listener.

This is a stereo radio cassette recorder. It has twin tape decks for tape-to-tape recordings. It has four loudspeakers, two for each stereo channel. The smaller speaker of each pair reproduces the higher-frequency sounds.

The units in this racked hi-fi system are perfectly matched for the best possible sound reproduction. At the top is an ordinary record player, and at the bottom a compact disc player. The unit also features a tape deck for playing tape recordings, an amplifier, and a tuner for receiving radio broadcasts.

Getting it Taped

These days, perhaps the most popular way of listening to recorded music is on a cassette recorder. This is a small tape recorder that plays a narrow tape wound on spools inside a handy plastic cassette. It has replaced the older type of tape recorder, which used a much wider tape that had to be threaded from spool to spool. However, such 'open-reel' tape recorders are still used in recording studios.

The tape used for recording is a ribbon of plastic coated with a thin layer of usually iron oxide or chromium oxide particles. The particles in the layer can readily be magnetized. When they are, they form an invisible pattern on the tape.

Any sound recording begins with sound waves entering a microphone. The waves cause a device in the microphone to vibrate. These vibrations are then changed into varying electrical signals, which represent the sounds. In a tape recorder, these signals are fed to a recording head. This consists of an electric coil device known as an electromagnet, which changes the electrical signals into varying magnetic ones.

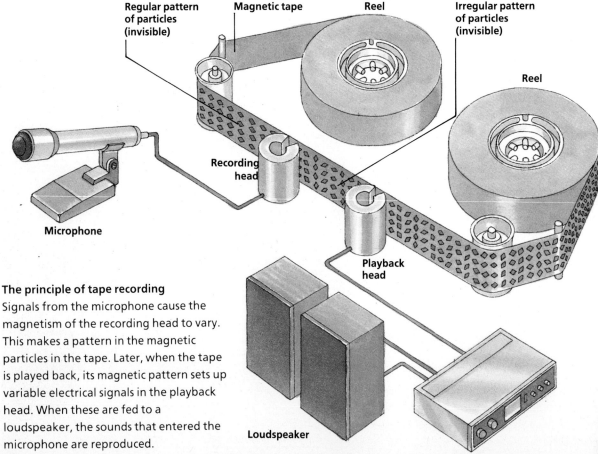

Regular pattern of particles (invisible)

Magnetic tape

Reel

Irregular pattern of particles (invisible)

Reel

Recording head

Microphone

Playback head

Loudspeaker

The principle of tape recording
Signals from the microphone cause the magnetism of the recording head to vary. This makes a pattern in the magnetic particles in the tape. Later, when the tape is played back, its magnetic pattern sets up variable electrical signals in the playback head. When these are fed to a loudspeaker, the sounds that entered the microphone are reproduced.

Sound waves to magnetic images

The magnetic tape goes past the recording head. As it does so, its oxide particles become arranged into patterns that represent the magnetic signals coming from the head. These signals represent the electrical signals from the microphone, which in turn represent the sound that went into it. So the magnetic pattern on the tape is a recorded 'image' of that original sound.

The opposite sequence of changes occurs when the tape is played back on the tape recorder. As the tape moves past a playback head its magnetic pattern changes the magnetism in an electric coil in the head. This sets up varying electrical signals, which are then changed into sound waves by a loudspeaker.

The tape used in cassette recorders is only about 4 millimetres wide. It usually has space for only four recording paths, or tracks. The tape used in recording studio open-reel machines is up to 50 millimetres wide. It may be able to accommodate as many as 32 tracks!

Recording studios always record the sound on tape first, even if they are going to make disc recordings (see page 14). These days a piece of music is not usually recorded all at once. Often the song, symphony or whatever is split up into parts – for example, rhythm guitars, drums, brass, vocal – and each part is recorded on separate tracks of the tape. The studio producer then uses a complicated machine called a sound mixer and blends the various tracks into one. In this way he can achieve a perfect balance between the instruments and singers.

The most popular kind of tape recorder these days is the cassette recorder. One of the smallest is the personal stereo cassette player shown here. It is equipped with headphones.

In contrast to the personal player is the open reel-to-reel tape recorder used in music recording studios. This machine can record 24 tracks on each tape.

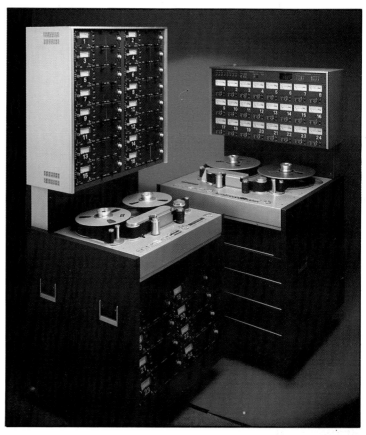

Singles and LPs

Before cassette tape recorders became popular, most people listened to recorded music at home on a gramophone, or record player. This is the modern version of Edison's phonograph (see page 10). For the record player, sound recordings are made on a plastic disc. On the disc there is a fine groove which spirals from the edge into the middle. In this groove the sound signals are 'stored'.

The record disc is a plastic copy of an original 'master' disc produced by the recording studio. The recording apparatus is rather like a record player. A master disc coated with lacquer is spun on a turntable. A chisel-shaped needle, or stylus, rests on the disc. Signals from the studio microphone are fed to the stylus and make it vibrate, cutting a wavy groove in the lacquer as the disc rotates. The wave pattern in the groove depends on the pattern of microphone signals, which in turn depends on the pattern of sounds entering the microphone.

In the groove

Playing back a record disc on a record player is the reverse process. The disc is spun on the turntable at the same speed as it was recorded. The stylus of the 'pick-up' head is then placed in the groove. As it passes along the wavy groove, it is made to vibrate. The vibrations are changed into electrical signals. When these are fed to a loudspeaker, the original sounds are reproduced.

Most 'singles' are played on the turntable at 45 revolutions per minute (rpm). LPs (long-playing records) are played at $33\frac{1}{3}$ rpm. Most records these days are stereophonic, or in stereo (see page 11). On the discs, the 'right' and 'left' sounds are recorded on different sides of the groove.

Cutting the master disc
A master disc being produced on a cutting lathe at the recording studio.

Producing the stamper
A 'negative' disc, or stamper, is made from the master disc by a series of electroplatings.

Recording on disc

These days disc recordings are not made directly from a microphone. They are produced from a pre-recorded tape (see page 13). Signals from the tape are then fed to a stylus and make it vibrate. The stylus, which is heated, cuts a wavy groove in a coating of lacquer on the master disc.

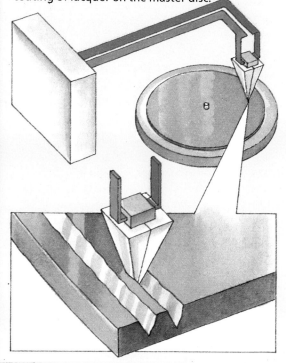

The record player

The two main parts of the record player are the turntable and the pick-up. The turntable is spun by electric motor, either by wheels or by a belt. It is made quite heavy, which helps keep its speed steady. The pick-up arm has a cartridge at one end and a counterweight at the other. The cartridge holds the needle, or stylus, which picks up the signals from the record groove.

Pressing the disc

The stampers (one for top, one for bottom) then squeeze a lump of PVC plastic to form the disc.

Testing the disc

After pressing, the disc is trimmed and then checked for faults on this automatic machine.

Digital Discs

If you want the very best sound quality from a recording, you have to buy a compact disc. This looks, and is, totally different from an ordinary black plastic disc. Compared with ordinary long-playing records, compact discs are tiny – only 12 centimetres in diameter. But they play for up to an hour. They are silvery in colour and have a transparent plastic coating.

Compact discs produce sounds of much greater fidelity because of the way sound is stored on them. On ordinary records, the sound is stored in the form of a wavy groove (see page 14). The waveform in the groove is similar to the waveform of the electrical signals coming from the recording microphone. But it is not identical, and therefore reproduction is not perfect.

Binary codes and laser beams

When making compact discs, the microphone signals are first changed into digital form – into numbers. Each and every part of a signal is given a precise value, so the whole of it can be represented *exactly*. As with computers, the numbers are expressed in a binary code of 0s and 1s. The numbers representing the signals are then recorded. This is done by cutting microscopic pits into the surface of a metal disc with a laser beam. The 0s are represented by the pits and the 1s by the flat surface. Together they form an exact record of the sound signals.

On the compact disc player, the disc is played back using a laser beam again. The beam is scattered by the pits and reflected by the flat surface. The reflected beam is picked up by a photocell. This device produces pulses of current (1) when stimulated by light from the flat surface, but no current (0) in the absence of light from the pits. Thus, the numbers of the recorded signals are reproduced exactly. They are then changed back into electrical signals, which are identical to those that came from the microphone. When these signals are fed to a loudspeaker, the original sounds are reproduced perfectly.

A similar kind of process can be used to record pictures. The result is the video disc. It is played back through an ordinary television set. The video disc is much bigger than a compact disc and is played at speeds up to 1500 revolutions per minute, three times as fast as a compact disc.

Signals from the microphone can be represented by a series of numbers (digits), and it is these numbers that form the basis of the recording.

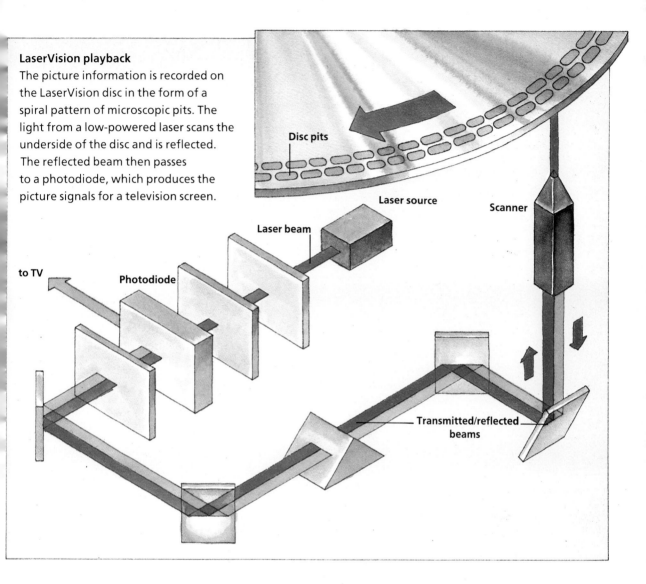

LaserVision playback

The picture information is recorded on the LaserVision disc in the form of a spiral pattern of microscopic pits. The light from a low-powered laser scans the underside of the disc and is reflected. The reflected beam then passes to a photodiode, which produces the picture signals for a television screen.

Disc pits

Laser source

Scanner

Laser beam

to TV

Photodiode

Transmitted/reflected beams

A LaserVision player and videodisc. The coded picture signals on the disc are read by a laser beam.

One of the latest compact disc players, which can be controlled by a remote-control unit. The sound reproduction is excellent.

TV Eye

The world's first regular black-and-white television programme service was started by the BBC in 1936; the first regular colour service by CBS New York as recently as 1951.

Today we take the television for granted, expecting when we switch on the television receiver, or TV set, to see good clear pictures in full colour on several channels. But we must not forget what complicated processes are involved in getting that perfect picture to the screen.

First the scene to be televised is viewed by the TV camera. The camera changes the light signals it receives into a series of electrical signals. These signals go to a transmitter and are broadcast over the air. At home the TV aerial picks up these signals and feeds them into the TV set, where they are converted into a picture on the screen (see page 20).

Picture signals

Inside the TV camera a lens produces a light-image of the scene viewed. The camera 'tube' changes the pattern of light in the image into a pattern of electrical charges on a plate. Then an electron 'gun' fires a beam of electrons at the plate, crossing it in a series of lines from left to right and from top to bottom. This process is called scanning.

The strength of the beam of electrons reflected back from the plate varies according to the pattern of charges. In other words, it represents the pattern of light in the original scene. It becomes the picture signal. This signal then goes to a transmitter for broadcasting. But before it can be broadcast it must be combined with, or carried

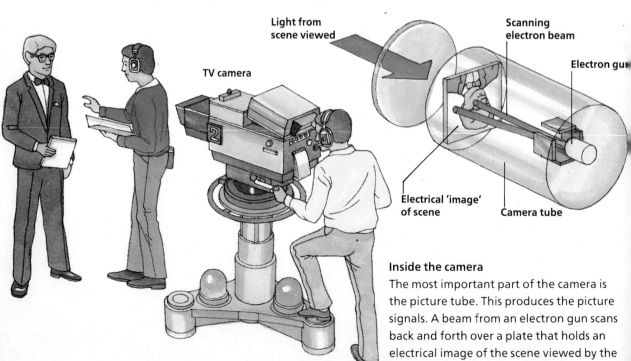

Light from scene viewed

TV camera

Scanning electron beam

Electron gun

Electrical 'image' of scene

Camera tube

Inside the camera

The most important part of the camera is the picture tube. This produces the picture signals. A beam from an electron gun scans back and forth over a plate that holds an electrical image of the scene viewed by the lens.

by, a radio wave, because only radio waves can be sent over the air.

In practice a TV camera usually has three tubes. Three are usually needed to transmit colour pictures. One tube picks up all the red in the scene viewed, one the blue, and the other the green. Picture signals representing these colours are then transmitted by carrier waves.

Daily television news broadcasts are transmitted 'live' from the studio.

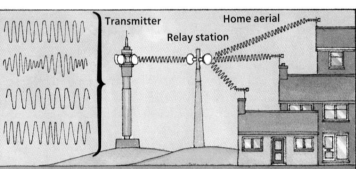

Transmitting the picture
The picture signals that come from a TV camera tube are transmitted through the air by a radio wave, called a carrier wave. The signals are made to alter, or modulate, the carrier wave in a characteristic way. A different carrier wave carries the sound signals.

Transmitter

Relay station

Home aerial

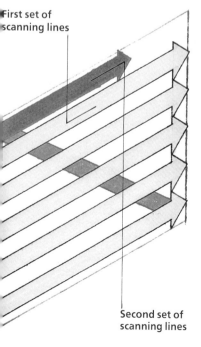

First set of scanning lines

Second set of scanning lines

Scanning
The beam from the electron gun in the camera tube scans across the plate from left to right in a series of lines. It does this in two stages. First it scans every other line. Then it goes back and scans the lines in between. In Britain 625 scanning lines are used, and 25 complete images are scanned every second.

Colour mixing
Colour television works because any colour can be produced from a mixture of three colours, the so-called primary colours red, blue and green. In a TV camera, filters are used to separate the different colours in a scene, which are then fed to separate camera tubes.

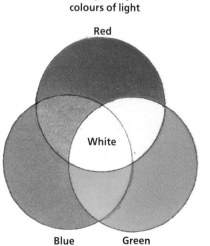

The primary colours of light

Red

White

Blue

Green

On the Screen

Most of us receive our TV signals through the air. And we need a suitable aerial to pick them up. The aerial consists of a number of short rods set one behind the other on a long horizontal rod. Only one rod, called a dipole, picks up the signal. The rods in front of it (directors) and a reflector behind it help amplify, or strengthen, the signals.

The TV signals travel from the aerial into the TV set. Electronic circuits inside the set first amplify the signals. Then they separate the signals representing the transmitted pictures from the radio wave carrying them (see page 19). The picture signals are finally fed to the most important part of the TV receiver, the picture tube. Its proper name is a cathode-ray tube, or CRT.

The simplest picture tube is the one used in a black-and-white TV set. It is a tube broad at one end and narrow at the other. It is evacuated, which means that most of the air has been removed from it. The inside of the broad end has a fluorescent coating. We see this as the screen. In the narrow end is an electron gun, which 'fires' a beam of electrons at the screen. When the

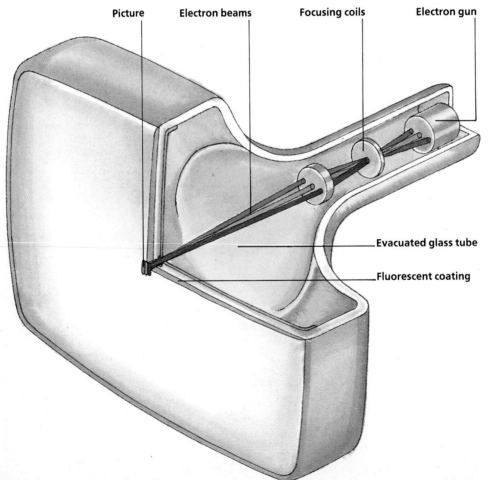

Picture   Electron beams   Focusing coils   Electron gun

Evacuated glass tube

Fluorescent coating

In the TV receiver the picture signals that come from the transmitter are fed to the picture tube. In this tube an electron gun shoots beams of electrons at a fluorescent screen, and causes it to glow. By means of focusing coils, the beams are made to scan in a series of lines from left to right across the screen, and from top to bottom, just as the ones in the camera tube did. In this way the picture is built up line by line. Note how thick the picture tube is. This is to resist the outside air pressure.

electrons hit a spot on the screen, they cause it to glow.

A spotty picture

The TV picture signals are fed to the electron gun and to magnetic coils around the tube. The signals fed to the coils cause the beam to scan, or move back and forth, across the screen in lines from top to bottom. This imitates what happened originally in the TV camera. If you look closely, you can see these lines on your TV screen.

At the same time, the signals fed to the electron gun alter the strength of the electron beam. This causes the brightness of a spot on the

screen to change. The result of all this is that a pattern of bright or dark spots appears on the screen. To our eyes, the spots all merge together to form the TV picture.

The colour TV tube generally has three electron guns. They fire beams of electrons representing the redness, blueness and greenness of the picture. The beams go through a so-called shadow mask, which ensures that they hit particular spots on the screen. The red beam hits spots which turn red; the blue beam hits spots which turn blue, and so on. When viewed from a distance, the colours merge together to create a true full-colour picture.

A selection of dipole aerials. The ones with the short rods are designed to pick up TV signals. Most of the rods are directors, which help direct the signals to the receiving rod, or dipole. The aerials with the longer rods are designed for receiving VHF (very high frequency) signals. They have a dipole in the centre.

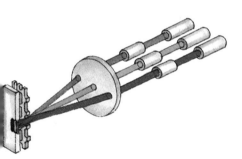

In many colour TV receivers the picture tube contains three electron guns, one each for the three colour signals.

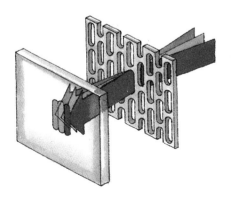

The 'colour' beams pass through a shadow mask, which ensures that they hit spots (phosphors) that turn the right colour.

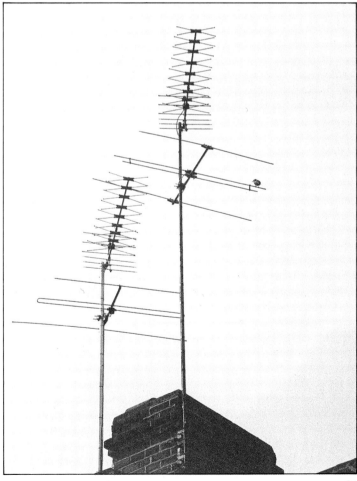

In the Studio

Most television programmes are put together in and broadcast from a studio. For elaborate productions, such as a historical drama, great resources are required – extensive scenery, expensive costumes, perhaps a huge cast of actors. Several cameras will be on hand to 'shoot' from different angles. The studio will be as crowded 'off camera' as 'on', with the stage

In the control room during the broadcast of the Independent Television News (ITN). Shots from various cameras and taped recordings appear on the monitor in front of the director and his staff. He chooses which shots to broadcast.

manager, floor manager, lighting technicians and numerous assistants.

Elsewhere in the studio, sitting in a darkened production control room, is the director. He or she and a team of assistants sit at a control console. In front of them are a number of television screens, or monitors. Pictures from the various cameras in the studio appear on some of the monitors. The director selects which picture he or she wants at any time. A person called the vision mixer then switches through that picture for transmission, and it appears on the transmission monitor.

Recorded and live programmes

Most programmes are not sent out 'live' as they are made, but are recorded first on videotape on a machine called a videotape recorder, or VTR. The tape is usually then edited, which means that certain parts of the programme are taken out or replaced to produce a perfect recording of the correct playing time.

Among the regular programmes that are sent out 'live' is the *News and Weather*. This looks a simple enough programme to produce, but in practice all manner of things can and do go wrong. The newscasters have a script to read and are also helped by a teleprompt. This is most commonly a small TV screen, placed beneath the camera lens, on which the words they have to say are displayed in big letters. The newscasters can look into the camera as they are speaking, without forgetting their lines. To us, it looks as if they know the news by heart, but they don't!

In the studio during the broadcast of the local News and Weather. On camera are the weather forecaster (right) and the weather map (left). Note the floodlights overhead.

On the videotape recorders, left, programmes are edited before they are broadcast. The parts of the original programmes that are wanted are re-recorded on another tape.

Outside Broadcasts

Some of the most spectacular live television viewing concerns events that take place outside the studio, such as the Olympic Games and the State Opening of Parliament. Such television programmes are called outside broadcasts (OBs). For big events, OBs require a great deal of forward planning to ensure that everything will go smoothly.

But televising even, say, a Formula 1 motor race is quite demanding. Several TV cameras are set up along the circuit at the start and finish points, at tricky bends, at the pits, and so on. The production crew choose the camera positions to cover the parts of the circuit where they think the most exciting action will take place. Some of the cameras may be mounted on hydraulic lift platforms to get high angle shots. Others may be carried in helicopters, or even in airships.

On race-day the production crew work in a mobile control room at the circuit that is a smaller version of the control room in the TV

A camera car and a mobile control room used for outside broadcasts. The camera car has a camera mounted on the roof. It is often used, for example, at horse-racing and motor-racing circuits to take action shots from different locations. The camera signals are transmitted to the mobile control room directly or via a link van. In the control room the programme director and staff view the shots from the various cameras on monitor screens, and choose which ones will be transmitted.

The Wimbledon lawn tennis championships are one of the outside broadcasting highlights of the year in England. The dish being erected here will beam the signals from the cameras on court to the TV studio for transmission.

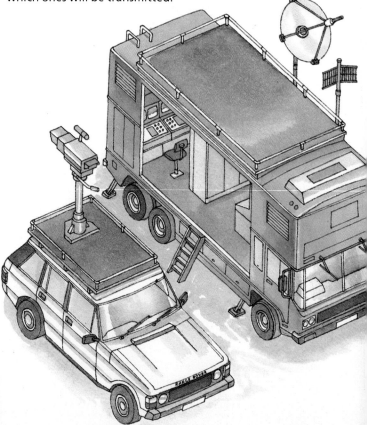

studio. They sit in front of a panel of TV monitors, each of which shows a picture from one of the cameras along the circuit track. Picture signals from the cameras often come into the control room via a radio link. In charge of the operation is the programme director, who selects one of the camera pictures for transmission. Over the radio, or by intercom, he or she also tells the cameramen what shots to take.

Finally the selected picture is transmitted to the TV studio via an aerial on a so-called link van next to the mobile control room. Or it may go by underground cable, or land-line.

Small-scale productions

For 'instant' outside broadcasting, such as on-the-spot news reports, there is a very much simpler OB set-up, involving perhaps only two or three people. There is usually a reporter; a cameraman, who carries a portable video camera on his shoulder; and a sound recordist, who carries the microphone and a portable videotape recorder. This form of news coverage is often called electronic news gathering (ENG).

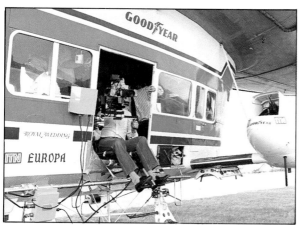

The Goodyear airship 'Europa' is often used as a TV camera platform for spectacular aerial shots.

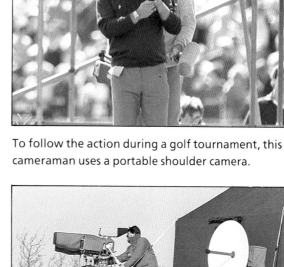

To follow the action during a golf tournament, this cameraman uses a portable shoulder camera.

A BBC TV cameraman shoots scenes during the wedding of the Prince and Princess of Wales in 1981.

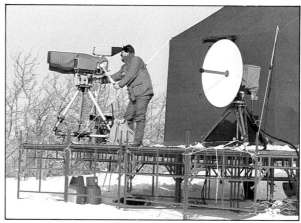

Filming the Winter Olympics at Sarajevo in 1980. The broadcasts were relayed worldwide by satellite.

Closed-circuit TV

In many department stores and shops these days you can see small TV cameras mounted high up on the wall. The cameras are fixed in one position or pan slowly from side to side, keeping an eye on the customers. They are linked by cable to small television sets or monitors, usually in one of the offices. There, a security guard watches the screens to make sure none of the customers is shoplifting – stealing goods from the store.

This kind of small-scale television network, with the equipment linked by cables, is known as closed-circuit television (CCTV). And one of its main uses is for security. It is a particularly efficient way of keeping an eye on large premises, and avoids the need for a large security staff or patrols. It is widely used, not only in stores, but also in businesses, factories and banks.

In banks, the cameras are usually concealed and record what they see on videotape. Over the years many bank robbers have been 'caught in the act' by the TV camera and later identified from the recorded picture.

Security staff find closed circuit TV a boon. It gives them 'eyes' all over the place and enables them to spot prowlers and people behaving suspiciously. Here an intruder has been 'caught in the act' on screen.

Close-up views, traffic surveillance

CCTV has many other uses as well. It is useful for teaching and training . purposes in schools, factories and hospitals. Medical students, for example, can be provided with a close-up view of an operation as though they were standing by the side of the surgeon performing it.

Traffic controllers and police often use CCTV to keep an eye on the traffic flow. They have remote control television cameras located on busy trunk routes and in notoriously congested areas and watch the scenes from a central control room. When they see hold-ups developing, they can take action in good time. Remote-control CCTV also comes into its own in hazardous conditions, for instance where there is poisonous gas or radiation. Security forces use cameras mounted on remote-controlled vehicles to look for bombs.

Closed circuit TV is widely used by traffic police for keeping an eye on the flow of traffic, particularly on roads entering and leaving big cities. The cameras are set up at suitable vantage points.

This TV-eye robot is used by anti-terrorist forces to look for bombs in abandoned vehicles. Its TV camera is controlled from a safe distance and sends back its signals by wire to a monitor screen.

Home Video

Sometimes on television you find that there are two good programmes being broadcast on different channels at the same time. The question is, which programme do you watch? In the modern home the answer is, both!

You can watch both programmes thanks to another electronic device, the video cassette recorder, or VCR.

A stereo sound colour TV set and video cassette recorder. The VCR can record from, and play back through, the TV set. Both are controlled from the keypad.

Using a VCR, you can record one programme while you watch the other. You can then play back the recorded programme through the TV set just when you want. Also with a VCR, you don't have to miss your favourite TV programme if you have to go out when it is being broadcast. You can set the VCR to record the programme for you, using its built-in time switch.

But the usefulness of the VCR does not stop there. You can also buy or rent pre-recorded video cassettes of many kinds, from short videos of pop music to full-length feature films. You can buy equipment to make your own video films. You need a camera and a portable VCR. After 'shooting' your film, you can immediately screen it on the TV. You do not have to wait for it to be developed as you do with ordinary cine film. And you don't need a projector either.

Cameras and tapes

The video camera is a smaller version of the TV broadcasting camera (see page 18). It may be held in the hand or mounted on the shoulder. Most video cameras have a built-in microphone so that you can record sound as well as pictures. Some have an electronic viewfinder in which you see exactly how your picture will appear on the screen.

Video cassette recorders record the TV signals on magnetic tape (videotape), like an ordinary sound tape recorder does. But video signals take up much more space on tape than sound signals. Videotapes are therefore made wider than ordinary magnetic tape. And the signals are recorded on them in a different way.

Using a home video recorder. This model is fitted with a boom microphone so it can record sound as well as vision. The vision and sound signals are recorded on a portable videotape recorder.

A bank of videotape recorders in a broadcasting studio. They are of the open reel-to-reel type and use 5-centimetre wide videotape. This is four times the width of the tape used in video cassettes.

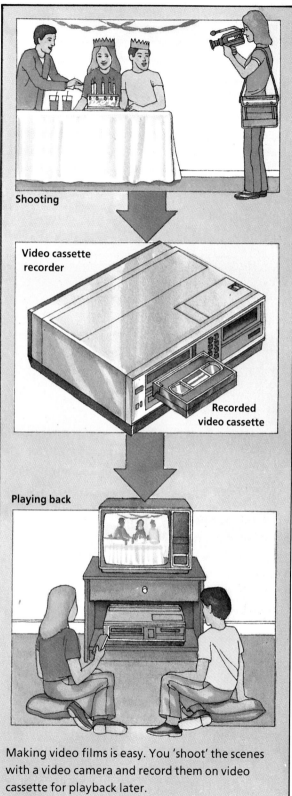

Shooting

Video cassette recorder

Recorded video cassette

Playing back

Making video films is easy. You 'shoot' the scenes with a video camera and record them on video cassette for playback later.

Screens Large and Small

For viewing at home, the ordinary 'small-screen' television set is fine. But it is really too small for a large group of viewers, say in a school or a conference room. The home TV screen measures up to about 70 centimetres from corner to corner. It is very expensive to make TV tubes with much bigger screens.

To overcome this problem, there are special projection TVs, which project the picture on to a separate screen. The screen can be many metres across. The most advanced kind of projector has three tubes which project images, via mirrors, onto the screen. Each tube projects a different colour, either blue, red or green. When the colours mix together on the screen, you get a true colour image. (This is similar to what happens on an ordinary television screen – see page 21.)

For more personal TV viewing, you can now buy a pocket TV. This has a screen only about 6 centimetres across. Some experimental wristwatch TVs have also been made with even smaller screens.

Projection TV
The most successful kind of projection TV uses three separate tubes to project red, blue and green images. These are reflected by a mirror on to the screen.

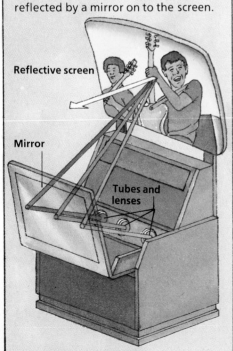

Reflective screen

Mirror

Tubes and lenses

Huge TV screens now form part of the visual attraction at pop music concerts in large arenas. They enable the audience to see better what is happening on stage.

Fluorescent or liquid-crystal screens

There are two main kinds of pocket TV, producing a picture in different ways. One kind uses a very flat TV tube. The picture is produced as usual on a fluorescent screen. The other type of pocket TV does not use a tube. Instead it forms pictures by means of liquid crystal display (LCD). This is the kind of display used in digital watches and pocket calculators. Different sections of the display turn black to form the digits and letters.

On the liquid-crystal TV screen the picture is built up from a very large number of tiny picture elements, or pixels. (Computer graphics are built up in a similar way.) When the TV signals are fed to the display, the pixels turn black, white or different shades of grey. The pattern of pixels forms the picture.

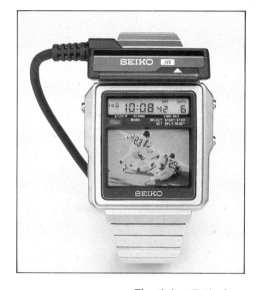

This pocket TV uses a miniature cathode-ray tube, which works in much the same way as the picture tube in an ordinary receiver.

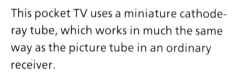

The picture on this pocket TV is formed by liquid-crystal display (LCD).

The tiniest TV is the watch TV, which has a liquid crystal picture. It is not practical for long-term viewing.

Cable TV and Satellite TV

In most parts of the world homes receive television signals over the air and collect them by means of an indoor or outdoor aerial. In large cities with tall buildings this kind of reception can be very bad. Many city homes therefore receive TV signals in a different way – by cable.

Cable TV is well-established in the United States, where some systems have been operating for more than 30 years. Nearly half the homes in the country have cable TV. In large cities like New York, viewers have the choice of up to 35 channels. The channels include national network programmes such as ABC and CBS and a variety of specialist programmes, which screen sport, music, drama, religion, children's entertainment, and the latest movie films. The viewers pay the cable TV company for the channels they watch.

Cable TV is only really just beginning in Britain, where only a few hundred thousand homes were connected by mid-1985. But its popularity is bound to increase as the great attraction is the large number of channels to watch.

New technologies, more channels
In a cable TV network, the TV signals are received at a central station and are then transmitted along cables into subscribers' homes. In the past, ordinary coaxial copper cables have been used. These are cables with an inner and outer conductor separated by a plastic sheath. Today fibre-optic cables are often used instead. They are able to carry more channels.

In the coming years the number of TV channels available to viewers is going to mushroom. This will happen because of direct broadcasting satellites (DBS). These are satellites far out in space that can broadcast programmes over whole countries. They are powerful enough to beam signals directly to the home. All you need to receive the signals is a small rooftop dish-aerial pointing in the right direction and a simple electronic converter.

The dish aerials at a cable TV station. They receive programmes via a communications satellite.

From the cable TV station, programmes travel to subscribers' homes by underground cable.

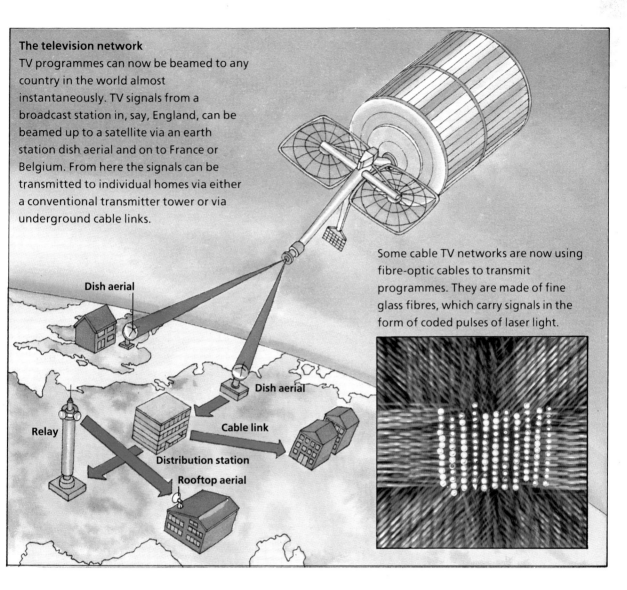

The television network

TV programmes can now be beamed to any country in the world almost instantaneously. TV signals from a broadcast station in, say, England, can be beamed up to a satellite via an earth station dish aerial and on to France or Belgium. From here the signals can be transmitted to individual homes via either a conventional transmitter tower or via underground cable links.

Some cable TV networks are now using fibre-optic cables to transmit programmes. They are made of fine glass fibres, which carry signals in the form of coded pulses of laser light.

Dish aerial

Dish aerial

Relay

Cable link

Distribution station

Rooftop aerial

In the station control room the programmes being transmitted are viewed on monitor screens.

Cable TV companies are able to broadcast dozens of different programmes at the same time.

33

Teletext

Nowadays the TV can provide much more than ordinary broadcast programmes. It can become a storehouse of all kinds of useful information – the latest traffic news, foreign exchange rates, airport flight times, local restaurant menus, what's on at the theatre, and so on.

There are two ways in which the TV can bring you this information. One is through the 'pages' of a TV 'magazine'. This method is called teletext. The other way is via a telephone link. This is called viewdata (see page 36). The general name for TV information services like teletext and viewdata is videotex.

Teletext signals are broadcast along with the normal TV signals. They appear in code in some of the spare scanning lines that are not used for making the picture on the screen. To view the teletext, however, your TV must be fitted with an electronic decoder. This converts the coded signals into a

Preparing material for broadcasting on teletext. Information for the teletext 'pages' is typed into a word processor, edited, and then fed into the controlling computer. When viewers at home key in a particular page number, the computer sends signals to their TV set, which displays the page.

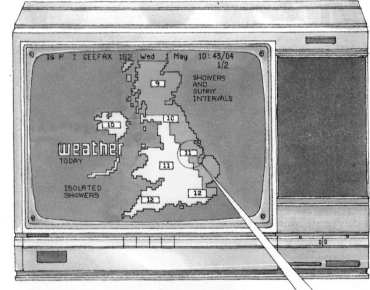

The weather situation over Britain is displayed in this teletext image. It uses simple graphics to show how the weather varies from place to place. The graphics are made up of combinations of coloured picture elements, or pixels.

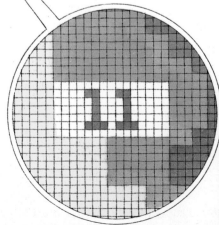

display of words and graphics. These are formed from patterns of tiny dots.

Selecting a page

To gain access to the teletext 'pages', you have a keypad, which is also the remote-control for the TV set. You press the 'Text' key, and an index page comes up on the screen. You then key in the number of the page you want. The pages of teletext are transmitted in turn, and you have to wait until the page you want comes up.

Because of this time lag, the teletext 'magazine' can only be up to a few hundred pages long. If there were many more pages, the waiting time would be too long.

The teletext system was pioneered in Britain, but is now operating in several other countries. The BBC were first with their teletext service Ceefax (from 'see facts'), which went on the air in 1976. Next came Oracle from Britain's independent TV network. The Canadians now have a teletext system called Telidon. The French have one, Antiope, and the Germans one, Videotext.

Viewers call up teletext pages on to their screens by means of a keypad. The pictures here show some of the services available.

Subtitles for the deaf and hard of hearing.

Wimbledon results for lawn tennis enthusiasts.

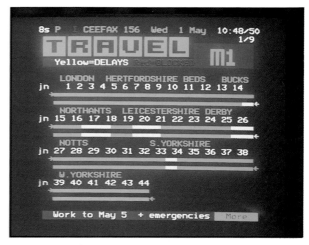

Traffic news for the motoring public.

Viewdata

The teletext 'magazines of the air' (page 34) have one great drawback. They are only a few hundred pages long. The alternative TV information service, viewdata, can give you access to hundreds of thousands of pages! The pioneering work on viewdata was done in Britain by the telecommunications part of the Post Office, now known as British Telecom. Their viewdata service, Prestel, began in 1979 and is still a world leader. Similar systems are now operating in over 20 other countries.

Viewdata is a system of bringing on to the TV screen information stored in a central computer. Communication between TV set and computer is along the ordinary telephone lines. TV sets must be fitted with a special adaptor, which changes the signals coming along the telephone lines into a form suitable for display on the screen. For business use, specially made viewdata terminals are available.

Adaptors can also be used to link home microcomputers into the network. In fact, Prestel runs a special magazine for microcomputer owners, called Micronet 800. It gives the micro enthusiast access to a huge library of computer programs and provides the latest microcomputer news and information.

Information at a price

As with teletext, you use a numbered keyboard to communicate with the viewdata system. Pressing a button on the pad switches the TV set to the viewdata mode and connects you automatically to the computer. You then key in the number of the page holding the information you require. Or you find the page number through an easy-to-follow index.

Unlike teletext, you have to pay for the viewdata service – you pay for the telephone and computer time. Many of the information pages are free, but you have to pay for specialist information. The 'information providers' put a price on each of their pages.

This is a special viewdata terminal for use in offices. Some terminals can record and print out viewdata pages.

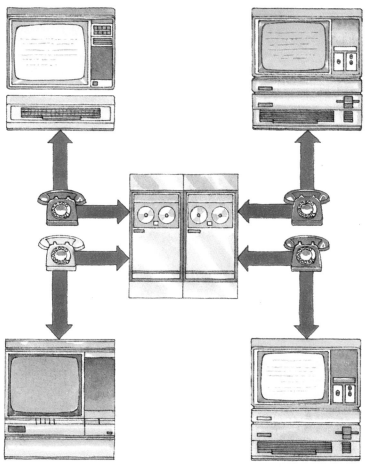

In a typical viewdata network a number of information providers, or service providers, feed pages of information into a central computer. A page is a screenful of information. The information is fed into the computer through the telephone lines. Information users at home, in business and in industry can extract pages of information, again via the telephone lines, and display them on their TV screens. Viewers find their way through the viewdata pages via a number of index pages.

People with microcomputers can tap into the viewdata network. This micro user is linked with Micronet 800, an electronic micro magazine.

A City broker checks on the latest share prices on Prestel's CitiService pages, which give information for investors.

Towards Tomorrow

On cable TV, viewers can take part in programmes. They can send simple responses using a keypad or keyboard.

Viewdata can give people access to unbelievable amounts of information, and its storehouse of information is expanding all the time. One way it does this is by linking up with other computer networks. But the viewdata network can do much more than just receive information. Because it uses the telephone lines, it can become a two-way system. We say it is interactive. Thus viewdata users can often communicate directly with organizations within the network. People can also shop from home. They call up shopping information on the screen, perhaps from a local department store. Then they order the goods they want by keying in order numbers and the number of their credit card. The goods are delivered in due course.

Viewdata users can send messages to one another through an 'electronic mailbox'. The messages are stored on the central computer until the person being 'written to' next taps into the network.

Cable TV can also be made to be interactive, if two-way links are installed. Viewers can then take part in some programmes. They can, for example, give their opinions on questions raised in discussions, or vote for acts in talent contests.

Travel agents are among the biggest users of viewdata. They can link up with the computers of all the major tour operators and airlines to get the latest information on holidays and flights throughout the world.

Home banking facilities are now provided by some banks and building societies through the viewdata network. You can check on your account at any time, and transfer money between accounts.

In three dimensions

Thanks to viewdata, teletext, home computers and cable TV, the role of the TV in the home is ever expanding. The technology of television is also improving year by year. Just around the corner is 3D TV. This is television that we view in three dimensions (3D), so that the picture appears to have depth. Two slightly different images appear simultaneously on the screen, one red, the other green. To view the image in 3D, you wear a pair of glasses with one red and one green lens.

Eventually a true 3D image visible without special glasses will be created by the technique of holography. True 3D still (as opposed to moving) images can already be created in this way.

Holography is an advanced form of photography made possible by the use of laser light. A laser beam is used to light an object, and its rays also fall on to a piece of photographic film. Light reflected by the object also falls on the film. The pattern made by the direct and reflected rays forms an image on the film, called a hologram. When laser light is shone through the hologram, a 3D picture of the object appears.

Holograms are now being increasingly used to store other kinds of information besides pictures. In a recent development, holograms are created on the faces (sides) of certain crystals. Different images appear as each face is illuminated by laser light. A crystal only a few millimetres across can store up to 1000 images!

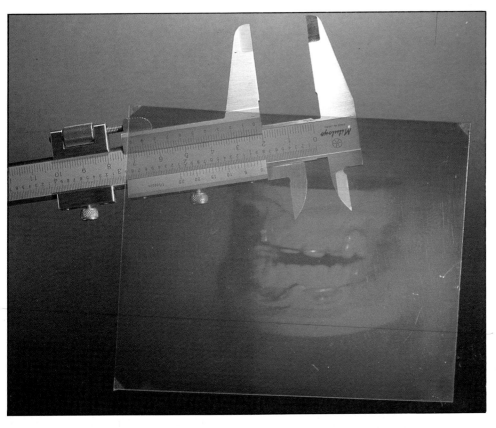

A holographic image of a dental plate. Accurate in 3D, each tooth can be measured.

Milestones

1877
American inventor Thomas A. Edison produces his first phonograph, forerunner of the modern record player.

1878
The English scientist William Crookes invents the cathode-ray tube, ancestor of the TV picture tube.

1884
Paul G. Nipkow in Germany develops a mechanical scanning device, consisting of a disc with holes in it in a spiral pattern.

1888
Emile Berliner in Germany demonstrates the gramophone, which uses flat discs to record sound, as opposed to the cylinders used by Edison.

1892
Berliner works out the modern mass-production method for making record discs – using a master disc and stampers. At first he uses hard rubber for the discs. In 1895 shellac replaces rubber.

1898
Valdemar Poulsen in Denmark invents the forerunner of the tape recorder – a machine that records sounds magnetically on steel wire.

1906
Boris Rosing in Russia produces crude pictures in a TV-type system using Nipkow discs.

1923
Vladimir Zworykin in the United States develops the first electronic TV camera tube, called the iconoscope.

1925
Bell Telephone Laboratories in the United States develop an electrical system of sound recording, using a microphone.

1926
John Logie Baird in Britain demonstrates a working TV System, using mechanical scanning by Nipkow discs.

1928
Baird and the American Herbert Ives demonstrate colour TV using Nipkow discs.

1935
The modern era of tape recording is introduced with the manufacture in Germany of coated plastic magnetic tape.

1936
The BBC open the world's first regular TV broadcasting from Alexandra Palace, in London.

1948
Plastic replaces shellac as the main material for making record discs. The grooves can be cut closer together, allowing the production of long-playing (LP) records.

1949
RCA in the United States demonstrates colour TV using a shadow mask, the system used today. But colour TV broadcasting did not begin regularly until 1951.

1956
Ampex in the United States build the first practical videotape recorder, able to record TV pictures.

1958
Audio Fidelity in the United States and Decca and Pye in Britain begin producing stereophonic records.

1960
The American scientist T. H. Maiman builds the first laser, later to be used in recording and playing videodiscs and compact discs.

1962
The communications satellite Telstar relays the first TV pictures across the Atlantic.

1969
The Apollo 11 astronauts make the first live TV broadcast from the Moon. Sony introduce the video cassette recorder in Japan.

1970
The first videodiscs are produced in Britain and Germany, but are not perfected until the early 1980s.

1973
In Britain, the BBC and the Independent Broadcasting Authority (IBA) introduce rival teletext systems, Ceefax and Oracle.

1975
The British Post Office telecommunications section (now British Telecom) introduces the world's first viewdata service, called Prestel.

1979
Matsushita invent a pocket-size flat screen TV, with a liquid crystal display (LCD).
Digitally recorded record discs become widely available.

Glossary

aerial — An arrangement of rods or wires used for picking up radio and television signals.

amplifier — An electronic device used to strengthen signals in audio and video equipment.

analogue — Something that is analogous (similar) to something else. The electrical signals that come from a microphone are analogues of the sound signals that enter the microphone.

audio — Relating to sound.

audiovisual — Relating to sound and vision.

cable TV — Television programmes transmitted via cables, not broadcast through the air.

carrier wave — A radio wave that 'carries' sound or vision signals from transmitter to receiver.

cassette — A device that contains ready threaded spools of tape and that slots into a tape recorder.

cathode ray tube — The correct name for the TV picture tube. 'Cathode ray' is another term for electron.

compact disc — A small record disc which is played back by means of a laser beam.

closed circuit TV — Television in which signals travel from camera to receiver by wire, usually over quite a short distance.

digital — A digital signal is one which is represented precisely by numbers.

direct broadcasting satellite — Or DBS; a communications satellite powerful enough to beam programmes into the home through a simple dish aerial.

electron gun — A device in TV cameras and picture tubes, which 'fires' beams of electrons.

electrons — Tiny particles of matter, found in all atoms. When they flow, they form an electric current.

hi-fi — Short for high fidelity, which means high-quality sound reproduction.

interactive TV — A TV system in which the viewer can take part. This is possible with cable TV and viewdata.

keypad — A hand-held unit with a keyboard used to control audiovisual equipment and to select pages on teletext and viewdata.

laser — A device that produces a very pure beam of light. It can be made to carry digital signals.

LCD — Short for Liquid Crystal Display; the kind of display seen on digital watches and calculators.

loudspeaker	The unit in audio equipment that changes electrical signals into sound. Usually just called speaker.
magnetic tape	Plastic tape used in tape recorders which has a coating (metal oxide) that can be magnetized.
microphone	A device in audio equipment which changes sounds into equivalent electrical signals.
monitor	A TV screen in a studio or control room on which pictures from cameras and videotape machines appear.
OB	Short for Outside Broadcasting.
optical fibres	Fine glass fibres sometimes used to carry communications signals.
Prestel	The name of British Telecom's viewdata service.
radio waves	Waves that can carry signals through the air.
remote control	A hand-held unit with keys, used to control audiovisual equipment from a distance. It works either by 'silent' ultrasonic sound waves or invisible infrared rays.
scanning	The process in a TV camera and picture tube in which an electron beam moves rhythmically line by line across a plate or screen.
stereo	Short for stereophonic. It usually refers to equipment that can reproduce sounds 'in depth' in a life-like manner, using two speakers, one on the left, one on the right.
stylus	A needle used to play back a record disc on a record player, or to cut the groove in a master disc when recording.
teletext	A system of calling up data on to the TV screen, via broadcast TV signals. It takes the form of a TV 'magazine'.
tuner	The part of an audio system that can tune into radio broadcasts.
VCR	Short for Video Cassette Recorder.
video	Relating to vision; or a video recording.
videodisc	A disc on which picture signals are recorded. It is played back by means of a laser beam.
videotape	Extrawide magnetic tape on which picture signals are recorded.
videotex	A system that can bring data on to the TV screen; usually teletext and viewdata.
viewdata	A system of calling up data on to the TV screen, via the telephone lines from a central computer.
VTR	Short for Video Tape Recorder.
waveform	A representation of the way a signal is changing.

Index

Acknowledgements

The editor would like to extend his grateful thanks to the many organizations and individuals who provided information and pictures for the book. He is particularly indebted to Neil Johannessen of Telecom Technology Showcase, Jane Marrow and Steve Lewington of TeleFocus at British Telecom Centre, and Joan Callieu, Kim Fitzsimmons and Sharon Cartwright at British Telecom International Publicity; to Malcolm Smythe, who created the visual presentation of his ideas; to Dee Robinson for the picture research – assisted by Francesca Wolf; and to Vivienne Canter who helped him develop the series idea when at Telecom Technology Showcase.

The designer would like to thank Graham Baylis at Dorchester Typesetting.

The Dataworld series of books was produced with the assistance of the Telecom Technology Showcase, British Telecom's exhibition, resource and information centre. Through a unique series of displays, videos and working models, Telecom Technology Showcase brings alive over 200 years of telecommunications history as well as offering a glimpse of the future of information technology.

Telecom Technology Showcase,
135 Queen Victoria Street,
London EC4V 4AT.
Telephone: 01-248 7444
Open Monday - Friday 10.00 – 17.00
Admission Free

PICTURE CREDITS
(T=top, B=Bottom, C=centre, L=left, R=right)
Pages 8-9 Bursten Marseller   11L & R Thorn EMI Ferguson   13T Thorn EMI Ferguson   13B FWO Bauch Ltd.   14-15 EMI Records Ltd.   17L Robin Kerrod   17R Bursten Marseller   19 ITN Picture Library   20 Thorn EMI Ferguson   21 Lionel Bender   22 ITN Picture Library   23T Marconi Electronics   23B Robin Kerrod   24 TeleFocus/British Telecom   25TL & TR ITN Picture Library   25BL & BR PYE TVT (Philips)   26 TeleFocus/British Telecom   27 British Transport Police: Ministry of Defence: 27B Lionel Bender   28 Intext (with permission of Richard Maybury)   29T Thorn EMI Ferguson   29B Marconi Electronics   30 Michael Rose   31T Seiko   31C Sinclair Research   31B Sony Ltd.   32T AT&T Bell Laboratories   32L, R, 33L, R Swindon Cable TV   34, 35TR, BL, BR Ceefax BBC TV   35TL Thorn EMI Ferguson   36 Prestel   37T Prestel   37BL TeleFocus/British Telecom   37BR Prestel   38 Swindon Cable TV: Prestel: TeleFocus/British TeleCom   39B John Walsh/Science Photo Library.
Cover photo: Bursten Marseller